ESSENTIAL
Maths

YEAR 6
BOOK 1

age 10–11

About the series

There are 18 maths books for children from 5–11 years old in the Essentials series. There are three Essentials books for each year. Each book in the same year contains the same twenty units or skills at a slightly higher level of difficulty. This means that throughout the year you can provide your child with appropriate essential maths skills which cater for progress, continuity and development.

How to use this book

Units

The book is divided into twenty different units. Each unit begins with a Remember box which introduces the unit and gives your child essential information. If possible discuss this with your child to ensure he or she understands it. This is followed by a number of activities to practise the skill and help your child use it effectively. By and large your child should be able to undertake these practice activities fairly independently but do help your child to get started on them if necessary. Remember to talk with your child about each unit and to support him or her as much as possible with positive praise as they work through the book.

Check-up tests

There are two tests in the book – a half-time and a full-time check-up test. The tests assess your child's progress and understanding of the preceding ten units. The tests may be marked by either you or your child. Your child should fill in his or her score for each test in the space provided so a visual record of progress may be kept.

Parents' notes

The parents' notes (on pages 28 and 29) provide you with brief information about each unit.

Answers

Answers to the check-up tests and units may be found on page 30 onwards. These may be used by you and/or your child to mark work done.

First published 2002
exclusively for WHSmith by
Hodder & Stoughton Educational
338 Euston Road
London
NW1 3BH

A CIP record for this book is available from the British Library.

Text: Paul Broadbent and Peter Patilla

Typeset by Fakenham Photosetting Limited, Fakenham, Norfolk

ISBN 0 340 85683 1

Printed and bound in the UK by Scotprint.

Year 6 Book 1

UNIT 1: **All about numbers**

REMEMBER

The **decimal point** separates **whole numbers** from **tenths**.

tens	ones	tenths	hundredths	thousandths
1	4 •	3	5	2
10	+ 4 +	$\frac{3}{10}$ +	+ $\frac{5}{100}$	$\frac{2}{1000}$

NOW TRY THIS

1. Write the value of the red digit.

a) 3.**68** _____

b) 14.0**5** _____

c) 28.**3**14 _____

d) 20.06**2** _____

e) 9.32**5** _____

f) 53.**7**09 _____

g) 0.05**4** _____

h) 31.6**2**4 _____

2. Write a matching decimal for each arrow.

a)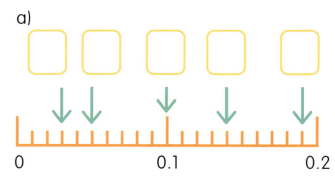

b)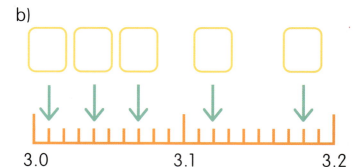

3. Rearrange this set to make a decimal number as near as possible to 1. There must be one digit in front of the decimal point.

6, 0, 8, 1, .

REMEMBER

To work out the **pattern** in a **sequence**, we look at the **difference** between each number.

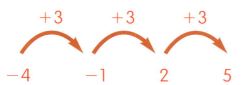

+3   +3   +3

−4   −1   2   5

The pattern or rule is +3

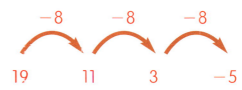

−8   −8   −8

19   11   3   −5

The pattern or rule is −8

Remember to include zero when you're looking at negative numbers in a sequence.

NOW TRY THIS

1. Write the missing numbers and the rule.

a) −16   −11   ☐−6   −1   4   ☐   Rule : _____

b) −15   ☐   ☐   18   29   ☐   Rule : _____

c) ☐   −2   ☐   −10   −14   ☐   Rule : _____

d) ☐   ☐   5   25   ☐   65   Rule : _____

e) ☐   0   −7   ☐   ☐   −28   Rule : _____

f) 40   28   ☐   4   ☐   ☐   Rule : _____

g) ☐   ☐   8   38   ☐   98   Rule : _____

h) 16   ☐   ☐   −11   −20   ☐   Rule : _____

UNIT 3: Measures

REMEMBER

Length, **weight** (or **mass**) and **capacity** are all measured using different units.

Length
1 centimetre (cm) = 10 millimetres (mm)
1 metre (m) = 100 cm
1 kilometre (km) = 1000 m

Weight
1 kilogram (kg) = 1000 grams (g)
1 tonne = 1000 kg

Capacity
1 litre (l) = 1000 millilitres (ml)
1 centilitre (cl) = 10 ml

We use **decimals** and **fractions** to show parts of amounts. For example:

$25 \text{ cm} = \frac{1}{4} \text{ m}$
$500 \text{ g} = 0.5 \text{ kg}$
$10 \text{ ml} = 0.01 \text{ litre}$

NOW TRY THIS

1. Complete these measures.

a) $3\frac{1}{2}$ m = _____ cm

b) 1.9 kg = _____ g

c) 14.2 cm = _____ mm

d) 0.25 l = _____ ml

e) 2.75 km = _____ m

f) 0.6 kg = _____ g

g) $4\frac{3}{4}$ l = _____ ml

h) 7.3 km = _____ m

2. Put in **<, >** or **=** to make each statement true.

a) 6.5 cm [ ] 650 mm

b) 6400 g [ ] $6\frac{1}{4}$ kg

c) 2300 ml [ ] 2.3 l

d) 82 mm [ ] $8\frac{1}{2}$ cm

e) 3.8 km [ ] 3750 m

f) 0.5 kg [ ] 50 g

g) 5.6 l [ ] 5060 ml

h) 580cm [ ] 5.8m

UNIT 4: **Data – line graphs**

REMEMBER

Line graphs have points plotted which are then joined with a line. There are many different types, but for all of them you must read them carefully:

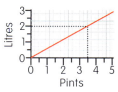

- go up from the **horizontal** axis to meet the line or point
- from this point go across to the **vertical** axis to give the value.

2 litres is approximately 3.5 pints

NOW TRY THIS

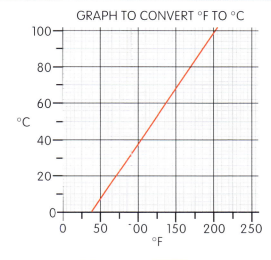

GRAPH TO CONVERT °F TO °C

1. Temperature is measured in degrees – Fahrenheit (°F) and Celsius (°C).
    This graph converts °F to °C.

    Use the graph to complete this table.

°F	50		150		65		90	
°C		80		25		30		42

2. This shows the average monthly temperature for Nice in France.

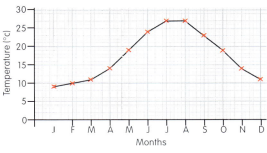

    Use the graph to answer these questions.

a) What was the average temperature in May? _____

b) In which month was the average temperature 23°C? _____

c) What was the difference between the hottest and coldest months? _____

d) Which month had the same average as March? _____

e) Which month was 5°C warmer than October? _____

UNIT 5: **Number facts**

You need to know all your **number bonds** to 20 for **addition** and **subtraction**.
Use this number grid to help learn the facts.
Use them to learn other trickier facts.

$7+8 = 15$
$17+8 = 25$
$70+80 = 150$

$15-7 = 8$
$25-7 = 18$
$150-70 = 80$

+	0	1	2	3	4	5	6	7	8	9	10
0	0	1	2	3	4	5	6	7	8	9	9
1	1	2	3	4	5	6	7	8	9	10	10
2	2	3	4	5	6	7	8	9	10	11	12
3	3	4	5	6	7	8	9	10	11	12	13
4	4	5	6	7	8	9	10	11	12	13	14
5	5	6	7	8	9	10	11	12	13	14	15
6	6	7	8	9	10	11	12	13	14	15	16
7	7	8	9	10	11	12	13	14	15	16	17
8	8	9	10	11	12	13	14	15	16	17	18
9	9	10	11	12	13	14	15	16	17	18	19
10	10	11	12	13	14	15	16	17	18	19	20

NOW TRY THIS

1. Write the missing numbers.

a)
$6+\boxed{} = 14$
$6+\boxed{} = 24$
$60+\boxed{} = 140$

b)
$9+\boxed{} = 16$
$9+\boxed{} = 36$
$90+\boxed{} = 160$

c)
$\boxed{}+8 = 15$
$\boxed{}+8 = 45$
$\boxed{}+80 = 150$

d)
$\boxed{}+4 = 12$
$\boxed{}+4 = 32$
$\boxed{}+40 = 120$

e)
$18-\boxed{} = 9$
$48-\boxed{} = 39$
$180-\boxed{} = 90$

f)
$15-\boxed{} = 6$
$35-\boxed{} = 26$
$150-\boxed{} = 60$

g)
$\boxed{}-4 = 7$
$\boxed{}-4 = 17$
$\boxed{}-40 = 70$

h)
$\boxed{}-5 = 7$
$\boxed{}-5 = 37$
$\boxed{}-50 = 70$

2. Use a timer. Answer these as quickly as you can.

a) $8+7 = \boxed{}$ b) $9-3 = \boxed{}$ c) $9+8 = \boxed{}$ d) $6+6 = \boxed{}$ e) $17-9 = \boxed{}$

$5+8 = \boxed{}$ $16-7 = \boxed{}$ $4+8 = \boxed{}$ $14-8 = \boxed{}$ $11-5 = \boxed{}$

$13-9 = \boxed{}$ $5+6 = \boxed{}$ $9+7 = \boxed{}$ $9-4 = \boxed{}$ $8+8 = \boxed{}$

$14-7 = \boxed{}$ $7+6 = \boxed{}$ $9+9 = \boxed{}$ $9+5 = \boxed{}$ $13-6 = \boxed{}$

Try it again. Can you beat your best time?

UNIT 6: **Fractions**

Fractions have a **numerator** and a **denominator**.

numerator $\longrightarrow \dfrac{3}{4} \longleftarrow$ denominator

Equivalent fractions are worth the same.
We usually write fractions using the smallest possible denominator.

These are part of the $\dfrac{1}{2}$ family.

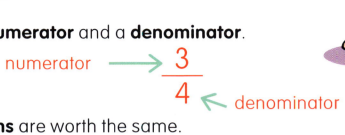

NOW TRY THIS

1. Complete these equivalent fractions.

a) $\dfrac{4}{\boxed{}} = \dfrac{2}{3}$

b) $\dfrac{2}{10} = \dfrac{1}{\boxed{}}$

c) $\dfrac{\boxed{}}{12} = \dfrac{1}{4}$

d) $\dfrac{6}{\boxed{}} = \dfrac{1}{2}$

e) $\dfrac{\boxed{}}{15} = \dfrac{1}{3}$

f) $\dfrac{2}{8} = \dfrac{\boxed{}}{4}$

g) $\dfrac{15}{20} = \dfrac{3}{\boxed{}}$

h) $\dfrac{9}{\boxed{}} = \dfrac{1}{2}$

2. Write three members of each of these fraction families.

a) $\dfrac{1}{3}$ ___ ___ ___

b) $\dfrac{1}{4}$ ___ ___ ___

c) $\dfrac{3}{4}$ ___ ___ ___

d) $\dfrac{2}{3}$ ___ ___ ___

3. Circle the odd one out in each set.

a)
$\dfrac{3}{5}$
$\dfrac{12}{20}$
$\dfrac{9}{15}$
$\dfrac{6}{10}$
$\dfrac{15}{20}$

b)
$\dfrac{9}{12}$
$\dfrac{12}{20}$
$\dfrac{3}{4}$
$\dfrac{18}{24}$
$\dfrac{6}{8}$

c)
$\dfrac{2}{6}$
$\dfrac{7}{21}$
$\dfrac{9}{24}$
$\dfrac{1}{3}$
$\dfrac{6}{18}$

UNIT 7: **2D shapes – quadrilaterals**

Quadrilaterals are any shapes with four straight sides.
Some quadrilaterals have special names and properties:

Square: 4 equal sides, 4 equal angles

Rectangle: 2 pairs of equal sides, 4 right angles

Rhombus: 4 equal sides, opposite angles equal, opposite sides parallel

Parallelogram: Opposite sides equal and parallel

Trapezium: One pair of parallel sides of different lengths

Kite: adjacent sides equal, one pair of opposite angles equal.

NOW TRY THIS

1. Name each shape. Tick any right angles.

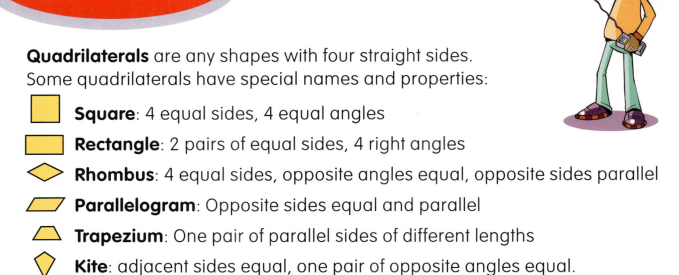

a)

b)

c)

d)

e)

f)

g)

h)

2. Draw three different quadrilaterals on this grid. Use a ruler and draw them as carefully as you can.

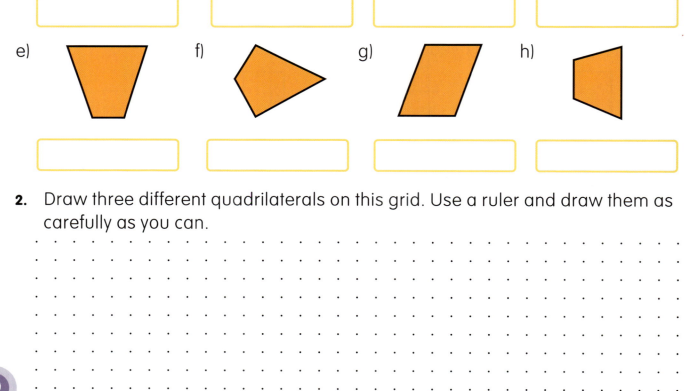

REMEMBER

am means ante meridiem which is in the morning.
pm means post meridiem which is in the afternoon.

Time tables and digital watches often use the
24-hour clock time. The 24 hour clock uses four digits.
8:35am is written as 08:35
8:35pm is written as 20:35

NOW TRY THIS

1. Write these as 24-hour clock times.

a) 7.20am [ ]   b) 4.15pm [ ]   c) 9.05pm [ ]   d) 11.30am [ ]

e) 1.40pm [ ]   f) 2.53pm [ ]   g) 6.03am [ ]   h) 3.48pm [ ]

i) 10.41am [ ]   j) 12.24am [ ]

2. Write these using am and pm.

a) 14:55 [ ]   b) 17:20 [ ]   c) 02:05 [ ]   d) 11:40 [ ]

e) 13:25 [ ]   f) 06:14 [ ]   g) 21:53 [ ]   h) 10:28 [ ]

i) 15:04 [ ]   j) 23:42 [ ]

3. Draw hands to show the times.

a) 18:55    b) 19:40 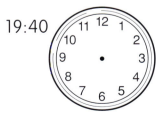   c) 11:35

d) 22:05    e) 14:20 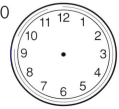   f) 07:50

UNIT 9: Addition

When we **add** numbers that are too large to total in our heads, we use a **written method**, like this.

```
  4209
  2833
+ 1694
───────
     6
───────
 1
```

For this method it is easier to start with the units $9+3+4 = 16$. Write the 6 and remember to add the 10 in the next column. This continues for each column to the thousands.

NOW TRY THIS

1. Answer each of these.

a)
```
  4198
+ 3206
──────
```

b)
```
  4734
+ 2966
──────
```

c)
```
  1877
+ 2091
──────
```

d)
```
  3072
+ 5637
──────
```

e)
```
  1897
+ 6794
──────
```

f)
```
  2785
+ 1934
+ 3497
──────
```

g)
```
  4105
+ 6783
+ 1346
──────
```

h)
```
  2155
+ 3905
+ 2086
──────
```

i)
```
  1037
+ 8489
+ 3856
──────
```

j)
```
  3267
+ 5409
+ 4564
──────
```

2. Write the missing numbers.

a)
```
  4 ☐ 7 2
+ 1 6 8 ☐
─────────
  6 0 5 ☐
```

b)
```
  ☐ 8 0 5
+ 3 9 ☐ 7
─────────
  8 8 0 ☐
```

c)
```
  ☐ 3 9 ☐
+ 1 ☐ 7 3
─────────
  9 2 6 7
```

d)
```
  5 3 ☐ 5
+ 7 ☐ 1 ☐
─────────
1 ☐ 7 6 0
```

e)
```
  5 2 7 7
+ 8 ☐ ☐ 4
─────────
1 ☐ 6 2 ☐
```

f)
```
  ☐ 3 2 ☐
+ 5 ☐ ☐ 5
─────────
1 2 3 0 2
```

3. Total three of these numbers to make 20,000.
There are two different ways. Can you find them?

a) ☐ + ☐ + ☐ = 20,000

b) ☐ + ☐ + ☐ = 20,000

6934   7020   3224   8379   4601   4839   9842

12

UNIT 10: **Subtraction**

REMEMBER

When we **subtract** numbers that are too large to work out in our heads, we use a **written method**, like this.

$$
\begin{array}{r}
3746 \\
- 1489 \\
\hline
\end{array}
$$

NOW TRY THIS

1. Answer each of these.

a)
$$
\begin{array}{r}
4725 \\
- 2876 \\
\hline
\end{array}
$$

b)
$$
\begin{array}{r}
6230 \\
- 4776 \\
\hline
\end{array}
$$

c)
$$
\begin{array}{r}
7060 \\
- 3652 \\
\hline
\end{array}
$$

d)
$$
\begin{array}{r}
7832 \\
- 2941 \\
\hline
\end{array}
$$

e)
$$
\begin{array}{r}
9400 \\
- 6575 \\
\hline
\end{array}
$$

f)
$$
\begin{array}{r}
10314 \\
- 3684 \\
\hline
\end{array}
$$

g)
$$
\begin{array}{r}
12319 \\
- 8675 \\
\hline
\end{array}
$$

h)
$$
\begin{array}{r}
23425 \\
- 12215 \\
\hline
\end{array}
$$

i)
$$
\begin{array}{r}
54196 \\
- 18652 \\
\hline
\end{array}
$$

j)
$$
\begin{array}{r}
47105 \\
- 29655 \\
\hline
\end{array}
$$

2. Write the missing numbers.

a)
$$
\begin{array}{r}
\boxed{}\,3\;7\;5 \\
- \;2\;\boxed{}\;8\;\boxed{} \\
\hline
4\;3\;8\;8 \\
\hline
\end{array}
$$

b)
$$
\begin{array}{r}
5\;\boxed{}\;6\;\boxed{} \\
- \;2\;8\;6\;5 \\
\hline
2\;1\;\boxed{}\;9 \\
\hline
\end{array}
$$

c)
$$
\begin{array}{r}
\boxed{}\,\boxed{}\;0\;1 \\
- \;3\;6\;4\;\boxed{} \\
\hline
2\;5\;5\;5 \\
\hline
\end{array}
$$

d)
$$
\begin{array}{r}
1\;0\;\boxed{}\;7\;\boxed{} \\
- \;\boxed{}\;5\;\boxed{}\;5 \\
\hline
1\;9\;0\;8 \\
\hline
\end{array}
$$

e)
$$
\begin{array}{r}
\boxed{}\,4\;3\;6\;\boxed{} \\
- \;7\;\boxed{}\;\boxed{}\;7 \\
\hline
2\;6\;6\;8\;4 \\
\hline
\end{array}
$$

f)
$$
\begin{array}{r}
4\;5\;\boxed{}\;\boxed{}\;4 \\
- \;1\;4\;6\;8\;5 \\
\hline
3\;\boxed{}\;3\;1\;\boxed{} \\
\hline
\end{array}
$$

3. Join the pairs of numbers with a difference of 5555.

4735   11200   10290   6830

3845   9400   12385   5645

Half-time check-up test

Check how much you have learned.
Answer the questions.
Mark your answers. Fill in your results.

SCORE

1. Write the value of each number.

1   1.1   1.2

a) ↑ a)   b) ↑ b)

a) [ ]   b) [ ]

/ 2

2. Write the missing numbers in this sequence.

| 17 | 9 | [ ] | [ ] | −15 | −23 | [ ] |

/ 1

3. Complete these measures.

a) 145 mm = _____ cm   b) 2650 g = _____ kg

c) 525 cm = _____ m   d) 6200 ml = _____ l

/ 4

4. This graph shows the conversion between Euros and pounds sterling.

1 Euro = 60p
What is the approximate value of:

a) €4.00 → _____

b) £6.00 → _____

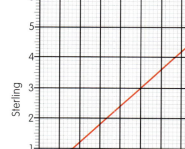

Sterling (y-axis: 0 to 6)
Euros (x-axis: 0 to 10)

/ 2

5. Write the missing numbers.

a) 39 + [ ] = 47   b) [ ] − 8 = 54   c) 70 + [ ] = 130

/ 3

14

6. Complete these equivalent fractions.

$$\frac{2}{\boxed{}} = \frac{\boxed{}}{30} = \frac{6}{9} = \frac{14}{\boxed{}} = \frac{\boxed{}}{45}$$

7. Join the names to the correct shapes.

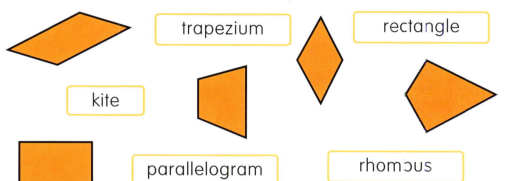

trapezium

rectangle

kite

parallelogram

rhombus

8. Convert these times.

12 hr	24 hr
7.25 am	
	19:50
3.32 pm	
	10:39

9. Work out the total.

$$\begin{array}{r} 8408 \\ +2355 \\ +3294 \\ \hline \\ \hline \end{array}$$

10. What is 4255 less than 9105? $\boxed{}$

UNIT 11: **Properties of numbers**

REMEMBER

A **multiple** is a number made by multiplying together two other numbers.
So the multiples of 3 are 3, 6, 9, 12, 15 . . . and they go on and on past 10 × 3.

There are rules to test whether a number is a multiple of 2, 3, 4, 5, 6, 8, 9 and 10.
For example a whole number is a multiple of:

3 – if the sum of its digits can be divided by 3
e.g. 615 (6 + 1 + 5 = 12), 4401 (4 + 4 + 0 + 1 = 9)

4 – if the last two digits can be divided by 4
e.g. 524, 680, 3312

6 – if it is even and divisible by 3
e.g. 738, 702, 516

> Do you know the rules for multiples of 2, 5, 8, 9 and 10?

NOW TRY THIS

1. Circle the odd one out in each set.

a) Multiples of 3

b) Multiples of 4

c) Multiples of 6

d) Multiples of 9

2. Write the numbers 100 to 120 in each of these Venn diagrams.

a)

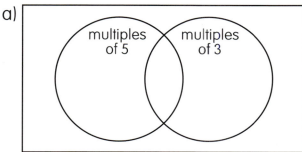

b)

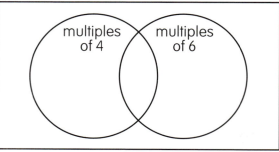

3. 360 is a multiple of many numbers. Tick the numbers that 360 can be exactly divided by:

2   3   4   5   6   7   8   9   10

UNIT 12 : Area and perimeter

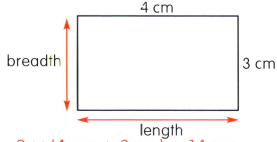

We can find the **area of a rectangle** by using a **formula**.

Area = length x breadth
    A = l x b

The **perimeter of a rectangle** can be calculated using this **formula**:

Perimeter = 2 x (length + breadth)
    P = 2(l + b)

Area = 4 cm $\times$ 3 cm = 12 cm^2 Perimeter = 2 $\times$ (4 cm + 3 cm) = 14 cm

4 cm

breadth

3 cm

length

NOW TRY THIS

1. Use the formulae to calculate the area and perimeter of each of these.

a)
4 cm
7 cm
area = _____ cm^2
perimeter = _____ cm

b)
6 cm
9 cm
area = _____ cm^2
perimeter = _____ cm

c)
4 cm
5 cm
area = _____ cm^2
perimeter = _____ cm

d) 3 cm
8 cm
area = _____ cm^2
perimeter = _____ cm

e) 2 cm
9 cm
area = _____ cm^2
perimeter = _____ cm

f)
6 cm
14 cm
area = _____ cm^2
perimeter = _____ cm

g)
9 cm
12 cm
area = _____ cm^2
perimeter = _____ cm

h)
9 cm
8 cm
area = _____ cm^2
perimeter = _____ cm

2. Answer these problems.

a) The length of one of the sides of a square is 6cm.
   What is its perimeter and area? Perimeter = _____ Area = _____

b) The area of a square is 81 cm^2. What is its perimeter?   Perimeter = _____

c) The perimeter of a square is 48 cm. What is its area?   Area = _____

UNIT 13: Multiplication

This is one way to work out 47 × 6 in your head:
Multiply the tens first, then the ones and add the answer together.

40 × 6 = 240
7 × 6 = 42

So 47 × 6 = 240 + 42 = 282

Decimals can be worked out in the same way:

3.6 × 8
3 × 8 = 24
0.6 × 8 = 4.8

So 3.6 × 8 = 24 + 4.8 = 28.8

It is always a good idea to work out an **approximate** answer first.

NOW TRY THIS

1. Answer these.

a)
30 × 4 = ☐

b)
50 × 8 = ☐

c)
60 × 3 = ☐

d)
90 × 2 = ☐

e)
70 × 6 = ☐

38 × 4 = ☐

57 × 8 = ☐

64 × 3 = ☐

93 × 2 = ☐

74 × 6 = ☐

2.

a)
79 × 3 = ☐

b)
84 × 6 = ☐

c)
95 × 4 = ☐

d)
47 × 8 = ☐

e)
63 × 9 = ☐

3. Calculate the area of these rectangles.

a)
3.8 cm
9 cm
area = _____ cm²

b)
4.7 cm
5 cm
area = _____ cm²

c)
6.8 cm
3 cm
area = _____ cm²

d)
9.2 cm
8 cm
area = _____ cm²

UNIT 14: Division

There are different ways to divide numbers.
Whichever way you choose it is always a good idea
to work out an **approximate** answer first.

$387 \div 4$ is approximately $400 \div 4$,
so the answer will be a bit less than 100.

```
        9 6 r 3              9 6 r 3
   4 | 3 8 7            4 | 38₂7
     − 3 6   (4 x9)
         2 7
       − 2 4  (4 x6)
           3
```

NOW TRY THIS

1. Use your own method to answer these.

a) $245 \div 3 =$ _____ b) $386 \div 5 =$ _____ c) $189 \div 4 =$ _____

d) $522 \div 6 =$ _____ e) $367 \div 5 =$ _____ f) $412 \div 8 =$ _____

g) $308 \div 9 =$ _____ h) $529 \div 4 =$ _____ i) $488 \div 3 =$ _____

2. Look at the numbers in the clouds.

(116) (677) (780) (425) (762)

Tip: Some answers may
have more than one
number.

Which of these numbers:

a) divide exactly by 4 $\longrightarrow$ _____

b) divide exactly by 5 $\longrightarrow$ _____

c) divide exactly by 6 $\longrightarrow$ _____

d) leave a remainder of 1 when divided by 4 $\longrightarrow$ _____

e) leave a remainder of 2 when divided by 5 $\longrightarrow$ _____

f) leave a remainder of 2 when divided by 3 $\longrightarrow$ _____

3. Write the missing digits 1 to 4.

a)
```
      7 □
  3 | 2 □ 6
```

b)
```
        8 3
  □ | 3 □ 2
```

1 2 3 4

REMEMBER

Don't confuse prisms and pyramids.

Prisms
The shape of the end gives the prism its name.
Slices of a prism are all the same shape and size.
Cuboids and cubes are special types of prisms.

Pyramids
The shape of the base gives the pyramid its name.
Slices of a pyramid are all the same shape but get
smaller to the point. The sices of a pyramid are always triangular.

NOW TRY THIS

1. Sort these shapes into prisms and pyramids.

a)   b)   c)   d)

e)   f) 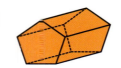   g)   h)

Tick the correct boxes.

Shape	a)	b)	c)	d)	e)	f)	g)	h)
Prism								
Pyramid								

2. Draw lines from each shape to the correct parts of this Venn diagram.

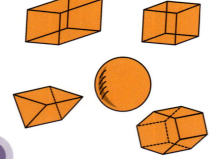

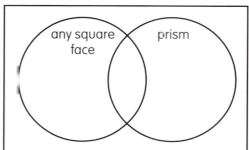

any square
face

prism

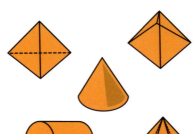

UNIT 16: **Position and direction**

A **coordinate** is a position on a grid. Negative numbers can be used to show positions.

The coordinates of A are (−3,4)
The coordinates of B are (3,5)

Read the **horizontal** coordinate first and then the **vertical** coordinate.

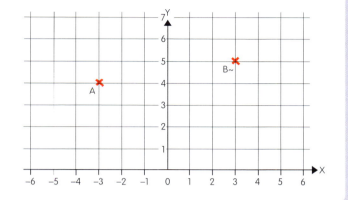

NOW TRY THIS

1. Draw two triangles at the following points:

   Triangle 1
   (−7, 3) (−6, 7) (−3, 2)

   Triangle 2
   (0, 2) (4, 7) (6, 1)

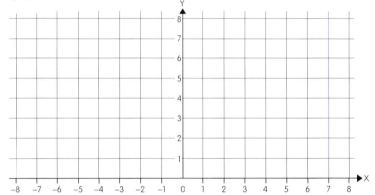

2. These are two corners of a quadrilateral.

a) What are the coordinates for:

   Position A _____

   Position B _____

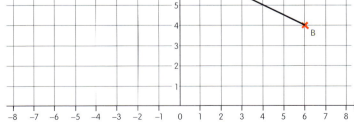

b) Plot the positions of the other two corners and draw the shape.
   The coordinates are:

   Position C ⟶ (−6,6)

   Position D ⟶ (2,2)

   Name the shape: _____

21

UNIT 17: **Decimals**

Try to remember these **fractions** and **decimals**.

$\frac{1}{2} = 0.5$ $\frac{1}{4} = 0.25$ $\frac{1}{5} = 0.2$ $\frac{1}{10} = 0.1$ $\frac{3}{4} = 0.75$

$\frac{1}{3} = 0.333\ldots$ $\frac{2}{3} = 0.666\ldots$

These two are **recurring** – they go on and on . . .

We can change decimals into fractions by dividing by 10 or 100. For example:

$0.4 = \frac{4}{10} = \frac{2}{5}$
$0.75 = \frac{75}{100} = \frac{3}{4}$

We can change fractions into decimals by dividing. For example:

$\frac{3}{5} = 5\overline{)3.0}\ \ 0.6$ $\frac{7}{8} = 8\overline{)7.000}\ \ 0.875$

NOW TRY THIS

1. Change these to decimals.

   a) $\frac{2}{5} =$ b) $\frac{7}{10} =$ c) $\frac{1}{8} =$ d) $\frac{4}{5} =$ e) $\frac{5}{8} =$

2. Change these to fractions.

   a) $0.9 =$ b) $0.3 =$ c) $0.85 =$ d) $0.15 =$ e) $0.01 =$

3. Join the fractions to the equivalent decimals.

   3.2 $3\frac{1}{4}$ 3.5   2.7 $2\frac{3}{4}$

   $2\frac{4}{5}$ 2.8 $3\frac{1}{5}$ $3\frac{2}{5}$ 3.4

   2.75 $3\frac{1}{2}$ 3.25 $2\frac{7}{10}$ 2.125 $2\frac{1}{8}$

UNIT 18: **Percentages**

Percent means 'out of 100' – **percentages** are **fractions out of 100**.
The sign for percent is %.
$25\% = \frac{25}{100} = \frac{1}{4}$

Numbers to be changed to percentages must be out of 100.
Example:
In a spelling test you score 8 out of 10.
$\frac{8}{10} = \frac{80}{100} = 80\%$

NOW TRY THIS

1. Change these test scores to percentages.

a) 7 out of 10 = _____ %   b) 15 out of 20 = _____ %   c) 20 out of 25 = _____ %

d) 34 out of 50 = _____ %   e) 19 out of 20 = _____ %   f) 15 out of 25 = _____ %

g) 3 out of 20 = _____ %   h) 23 out of 25 = _____ %

2. Complete each fraction.

a) $75\% = \dfrac{\boxed{}}{4}$ b) $20\% = \dfrac{\boxed{}}{5}$ c) $15\% = \dfrac{\boxed{}}{20}$ d) $90\% = \dfrac{\boxed{}}{10}$

e) $45\% = \dfrac{\boxed{}}{20}$ f) $25\% = \dfrac{\boxed{}}{4}$ g) $60\% = \dfrac{\boxed{}}{5}$ h) $98\% = \dfrac{\boxed{}}{50}$

3. Write the percentages given in these headlines.

a)
> There was a one-in-a-hundred
> chance of finding
> the diamond

[ ] %

b)
> Eight out of ten cats said they prefer
> fresh food to tinned food

[ ] %

c)
> Four in five people read our newspaper!
> The rest look at the pictures . . .

[ ] %

d)
> Fifty people were questioned
> and thirty-five of them provided
> useful information

[ ] %

e)
> Only eighteen
> of the twenty-five
> diners were satisfied
> with the food

[ ] %

f)
> Liverpool have won sixteen
> of their last twenty matches
> and are now favourites
> for the title

[ ] %

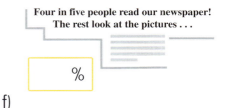

UNIT 19: **Symmetry**

A **line of symmetry** is the same as a mirror line.
One side of the line is the reflection of the other side.

These two shapes are a reflection of each other.

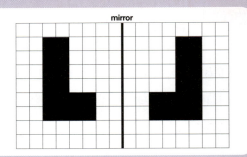

NOW TRY THIS

1. Draw the reflection of the triangle.

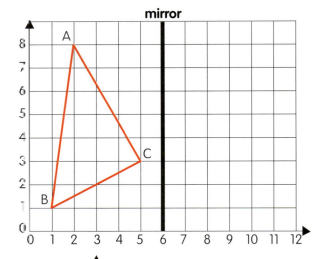

2. Plot these coordinates on the grid.

   A (5,7)   B (8,8)   C (5,5)   D (2,8)

   • Join them in order to make a quadrilateral
   • Draw the reflection of the quadrilateral.
   • Write the coordinates of the
     reflected quadrilateral

   (__ , __) (__ , __) (__ , __) (__ , __)

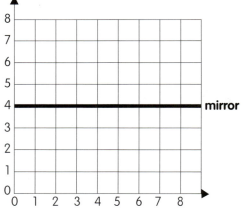

3. Draw a reflection of this pentagon.

   • Write the coordinates of the
     reflected pentagon

   (__ , __) (__ , __) (__ , __) (__ , __) (__ , __)

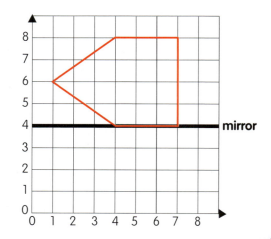

UNIT 20: **Money**

REMEMBER

When you **add** and **subtract money** make sure the columns are in line. The points should be underneath each other.

You can check subtraction by addition.

$$
\begin{array}{r}
£37.08 \\
- \quad £8.75 \\
\hline
£28.33 \\
\hline
\end{array}
$$

Check: £28.33 + £8.75 = £37.08

NOW TRY THIS

1. Write the change you would get from £50 if you bought each pair of items.

a)	b)	c)	d)	e)	f)
£9.56	£18.08	£18.63	£7.86	£13.28	£13.85
£17.45	£12.43	£8.58	£36.29	£21.93	£32.96
Change	Change	Change	Change	Change	Change
£	£	£	£	£	£

2. Solve this problem.

   The Lewis family are thinking about buying a family membership ticket for their local museum.

Castle Museum

Admission prices
Adults £2.30
Children 85p
Annual family membership £45

How many times would the Lewis family need to visit the museum for their membership ticket to be cheaper than paying at each visit? _____ times.

Full-time check-up test

Check how much you have learned.
Answer the questions.
Mark your answers. Fill in your results.

1. Circle the numbers that are multiples of both 3 and 4.

423   256   144   276   524   216

/1

2. What is the area and perimeter of this rectangle?

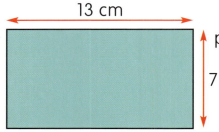

13 cm

7 cm

perimeter = [   ] cm

area = [   ] cm^2

/2

3. Answer these.

a) $76 \times 4 =$ [   ]

b) $5.4 \times 8 =$ [   ]

/2

4. Use your own method to answer these.

a) $364 \div 5 =$ [   ]

b) $831 \div 6 =$ [   ]

/2

5. Tick the odd one out in each set.

a)

     □

b)

□ □ □ □ □ □

/2

6. What are the coordinates of A and B?

A ➝ _____ B ➝ _____

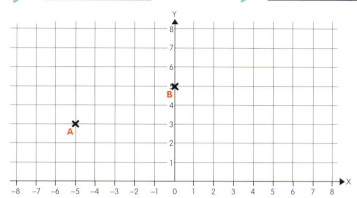

7. Write the equivalent fractions and decimals.

a) $\dfrac{3}{5}$ = [ ]

b) [ ] = 0.25

c) $\dfrac{7}{10}$ = [ ]

d) [ ] = 0.02

8. Change these fractions to percentages.

a) $\dfrac{3}{5}$ = [ ] %

b) $\dfrac{7}{20}$ = [ ] %

c) $\dfrac{39}{50}$ = [ ] %

9. Draw a reflection of the shape.

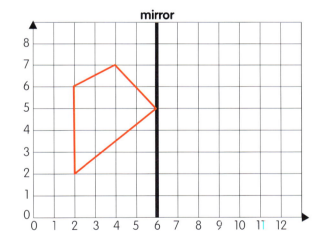

10. Answer this.
Liam bought three postcards and two posters from a gift shop.

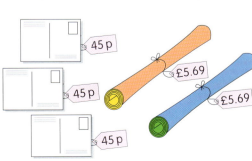

What change did he get from £20? _____

Parents' notes

Unit 1 – All about numbers
The place value is the position or place of a digit in a number. The same digit has a different value at different places in the number, either side of the decimal point. Children need to know the value of the decimal places: tenths, hundredths and thousandths. Relate these to fractions and that will help see how small these decimals are. A common error is to think that, for example, 0.2 is smaller than 0.18. Children need to see that 2/10 is bigger than 18/100.

Unit 2 – Number sequences
Number sequences are lists of numbers with a pattern between each number. Encourage your child to work out the difference between each number, as that gives the rule for the missing numbers. If negative numbers are involved, make sure that zero is included in the sequences.

Unit 3 – Measures
The metric system is a system of weights and measures. All the units in the metric system are in tens, hundreds and thousands which makes it a lot easier to convert between measures than the old imperial system. Millimetres, metres, millilitres, litres, grams and kilograms are all examples of units in the metric system. Check that your child is able to convert fractions of quantities, such as halves, quarters and tenths of centimetres, metres, litres or kilograms.

Unit 4 – Data – line graphs
Line graphs have points plotted which are then joined with a line. Encourage your child to read them by going up from the horizontal axis to meet the line and then from this point go across to the vertical axis to give the value. Make sure your child understands that the scale on graphs can alter. It is important to read all the information about each graph, such as title and axis headings so they have a good understanding of the graph.

Unit 5 – Number facts
Your child needs to be able to quickly recall all the addition and subtraction facts within 20. Once they know these they can then use them to work out other facts based on these. So, for example, once your child knows that $8+6 = 14$, they should be able to work out $80+60$, $18+6$, $38+6$, $800+600$…

Unit 6 – Fractions
Equivalence in fractions (such as $2/3 = 8/12$) is a very important concept for children to understand. Check that your child knows that the number above the line of a fraction is the numerator and the number below the line is the denominator. Look for the pattern between equivalent fractions. For example $2/3 = 8/12$. Compare the denominators and numerators and you can see that $2\times4 = 8$ and $3\times4 = 12$. Simplifying a fraction is making a fraction as simple as possible. So 4/20 can be simplified to 1/5.

Unit 7 – 2D shapes – quadrilaterals
Polygons are 2-dimensional shapes with straight sides. Each has a special name related to the number of sides, so any shape with four straight sides is a quadrilateral. There are many special named quadrilaterals with certain features. Look at the properties of the different shapes and try to recognise what makes, for example, a rhombus unique. Make sure your child recognises that some shapes may have more than one name. For example, a square is a special rectangle and also a type of parallelogram.

Unit 8 – Time
Children need to be able to relate the 24-hour clock to the 12-hour clock with am and pm. Remind your child that 24-hour time always has four digits. From midnight until midday (am times) the two times have the same numbers, eg 7.45am: 0745 or 10.25am: 1025. In the afternoon and evening (pm times) the 24-hour clock continues on from 1200 to 1300, 1400 etc. The time is, in effect, written with an extra 12 hours added, eg 2.15pm: 1415 or 9.35pm: 2135.

Unit 9 – Addition
When adding two numbers always encourage your child to look at the numbers first to see if they can be added mentally. If the numbers are too big, then they will need to use a written method. There are several different written methods, and this 'vertical' method is just one particular example. It may be that your child wants to make informal jottings of numbers as they are added or they may prefer the formal method shown. Go through each step carefully, making sure that the columns are lined up.

Unit 10 – Subtraction
As with addition always encourage your child to look at the numbers first to see if they can be subtracted mentally. If they need to use a written method they can choose between the formal method shown, or use their own method. The 'vertical' method is called decomposition, where tens and hundreds are exchanged to make the numbers easier to work with. An alternative is to find the difference between two numbers, counting on from the smaller number to the next ten and then on to the larger number. This is a more informal written method, similar to the mental method of counting on.

Unit 11 – Special numbers

Children need to recognise multiples of different numbers to 10. Make sure they understand that multiples don't stop at 10× a number, but go on and on. The important thing is to recognise the 'rule' for a set of multiples. These are called 'rules of divisibility', used to recognise whether a large number can be divided by, or is a multiple of, a certain number. For example we know that 717 is a multiple of 3 because the digits total 15 which is a multiple of 3.

Unit 12 – Area and perimeter

Children should be able to use the two formulae for working out the area and perimeter of a rectangle. Make sure your child understands that we use just the initial letters to represent the words, for example l is length and b is breadth. Check that area and perimeter aren't confused, and remind them that area is measured in square centimetres (cm^2) or square metres (m^2).

Unit 13 – Multiplication

The most popular method used to multiply a 2-digit number by a single digit is to break up (partition) the 2-digit number. So, for example, 36×5 is 30×5 (150) added to 6×5 (30). So 36×5 is 180. This can be done in any order, tens first or ones first. This is exactly the same when multiplying decimals, breaking it up into whole numbers and decimals and multiplying each part.

Unit 14 – Division

Written division methods are quite tricky, so it is important that your child is confident at dividing numbers mentally and knows their multiplication tables. This will help speed up the stages at working out a written division and allow them to concentrate on the process. Encourage your child to estimate an approximate answer first. Read through the long method where the number to be divided is broken up into hundreds, tens and ones, and then relate this to the short method. This will probably be the method that your child will want to use when carrying out written division calculations.

Unit 15 – 3D shapes

Your child will need to be able to recognise and name 3D shapes and describe their properties. This will involve counting the number of faces, edges and vertices (corners). Prisms and pyramids can cause confusion. A pyramid has triangular sides that meet at a point. The base shape gives its name, eg 'square based pyramid'. A prism has two end shapes that are identical and rectangular sides. A triangular prism has two triangle end faces and three rectangle side faces.

Unit 16 – Position and direction

A common error when reading co-ordinates is to get the two numbers the wrong way around. In the example position (3,5) is shown as B. Encourage your child to start at the zero and go across the horizontal x axis until it is level with the B (across 3) and then up to B (up 5). This will get your child into the habit of reading across the x axis before going up the y axis. It is the same for negative numbers, read across and then up.

Unit 17 – Decimals

Fractions and decimals are the same thing written in different ways, they are parts of a whole number. It is useful to be able to change fractions to decimals and the other way round. Encourage your child to learn all the tenths, so they know, for example that 3/10 is 0.3. They can then work out fifths, for example 2/5 is 4/10 which is 0.4. When converting fractions to decimals, the line in a fraction means 'divided by'. So written as a division: $3/8 = 3 \div 8 = 0.375$

Unit 18 – Percentages

Percentages are simply fractions out of 100. Children need to understand equivalent fractions (eg 20/100 = 1/5) in order to convert fractions to percentages and vice versa. To change fractions to percentages make them out of 100, for example 11/20 as a percentage is 55% (multiply numerator and denominator by 5). To change percentages to fractions write the percentage as a fraction out of 100 and then simplify. For example, 80% or 80/100 is the same as 4/5.

Unit 19 – Symmetry

A reflection is the image seen in a mirror. A shape with two sides that are mirror images has reflection or line symmetry. The co-ordinates grid needs to be used to work out the exact position of each reflected point. The best strategy is to count the number of squares from each point to the mirror line and then work out the same number of squares on the other side of the line. The result can be checked with a mirror.

Unit 20 – Money

When adding money amounts that are difficult to do mentally, make sure the columns line up so the decimal points are under each other. Then the normal written method for addition can be used. With subtraction or working out change it may be easier to use a 'shopkeepers method', even as a written method. This involves counting on from the cost of the item to the amount given, writing down the money amounts as you go along and totalling the amount of change.

Answers

Unit 1: All about numbers (page 4)

1. a) $\frac{6}{10}$ b) $\frac{5}{100}$ c) $\frac{3}{10}$ d) $\frac{2}{1000}$
   e) $\frac{5}{1000}$ f) $\frac{7}{10}$ g) $\frac{4}{1000}$ h) $\frac{2}{100}$

2. a) 0.03 0.05 0.1 0.14 0.19
   b) 3.01 3.04 3.07 3.12 3.18

3. 1.068

Unit 2: Number sequences (page 5)

1. a) −6 9 Rule: +5
   b) −4 7 40 Rule: +11
   c) 2 −6 −20 Rule: −4
   d) −35 −15 45 Rule: +20
   e) 7 −14 −21 Rule: −7
   f) 16 −8 −20 Rule: −12
   g) −52 −22 68 Rule: +30
   h) 7 −2 −29 Rule: −9

Unit 3: Measures (page 6)

1. a) 350 cm b) 1900 g c) 142 mm
   d) 250 ml e) 2750 m f) 600 kg
   g) 4750 ml h) 7300 m

2. a) < b) > c) = d) <
   e) > f) > g) > h) =

Unit 4: Data - line graphs (page 7)

1. Answers are approximate.

°F	50	176	150	77	65	86	90	100
°C	10	80	65	25	18	30	32	42

2. a) 19°C b) September c) 18°C
   d) December e) June

Unit 5: Number facts (page 8)

1. a) 8 b) 7 c) 7 d) 8 e) 9 f) 9
   18 27 37 28 9 9
   80 70 70 80 90 90
   g) 11 h) 12
   21 42
   110 120

2. a) 15 b) 6 c) 17 d) 12 e) 8
   13 9 12 6 6
   4 11 16 5 16
   7 13 18 14 7

Unit 6: Fractions (page 9)

1. a) 6 b) 5 c) 3 d) 12
   e) 5 f) 1 g) 4 h) 18

2. There are many answers but these are some possible answers.

a) $\frac{2}{6}$ $\frac{3}{9}$ $\frac{4}{12}$ b) $\frac{2}{8}$ $\frac{3}{12}$ $\frac{4}{16}$
c) $\frac{6}{8}$ $\frac{9}{12}$ $\frac{12}{16}$ d) $\frac{4}{6}$ $\frac{6}{9}$ $\frac{8}{12}$

3. a) $\frac{15}{20}$ b) $\frac{12}{20}$ c) $\frac{9}{24}$

Unit 7: 2D shapes - quadrilaterals (page 10)

1. a) square b) rectangle
   c) rhombus d) parallelogram
   e) trapezium f) kite
   g) parallelogram h) trapezium

2. Check that each shape is a quadrilateral.

Unit 8: Time (page 11)

1. a) 07:20 b) 16:15
   c) 21:05 d) 11:30
   e) 13:40 f) 14:53
   g) 06:03 h) 15:48
   i) 10:41 j) 00:24

2. a) 2:55 pm b) 5:20 pm
   c) 2:05 am d) 11:40 am
   e) 1:25 pm f) 6:14 am
   g) 9:53 pm h) 10:28 am
   i) 3:04 pm j) 11:42 pm

3. a) 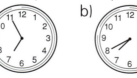 b) c)
   d) e) f)

Unit 9: Addition (page 12)

1. a) 7404 b) 7700
   c) 3968 d) 8709
   e) 8691 f) 8216
   g) 12,234 h) 8146
   i) 13,382 j) 13,240

2. a)
```
    4 [3] 7 2
  + 1 6 8 [5]
  ─────────────
    6 0 5 [7]
```
b)
```
  [4] 8 0 5
  + 3 9 [9] 7
  ─────────────
    8 8 0 [2]
```

c)
```
  [7] 3 9 [4]
  + 1 [8] 7 3
  ─────────────
    9 2 6 7
```
d)
```
    5 3 [4] 5
  + 7 [4] 1 [5]
  ─────────────
    1 [2] 7 6 0
```

e)
```
    5 2 7 7
  + 8 [3] [4] 4
  ─────────────
  1 [3] 6 2 [1]
```
f)
```
  [6] 3 2 [7]
  + 5 [9] 7 [5]
  ─────────────
  1 2 3 0 2
```

3. 3224 + 6934 + 9842
4601 + 7020 + 8379

Unit 10: Subtraction (page 13)
1. a) 1849   b) 1454   c) 3408
d) 4891   e) 2825   f) 6630
g) 3644   h) 11,210   i) 35,544
j) 17,450

2. a)
```
  [7] 3 7 5
  − 2 [9] 8 [7]
  ─────────────
    4 3 8 8
```
b)
```
  5 [0] 6 [4]
  − 2 8 6 5
  ─────────────
    2 1 [9] 9
```

c)
```
  [6] [2] 0 1
  − 3 6 4 [6]
  ─────────────
    2 5 5 5
```
d)
```
  1 0 [4] 7 [3]
  −   [8] 5 6 5
  ─────────────
    1 9 0 8
```

e)
```
  [3] 4 3 6 [1]
  −   7 [6] [7] 7
  ─────────────
    2 6 6 8 4
```
f)
```
  4 5 [0] [0] 4
  − 1 4 6 8 5
  ─────────────
  3 [0] 3 1 [9]
```

3. 4735 → 10,290   11,200 → 5645
6830 → 12,385   3845 → 9400

Half-time check-up test (page 14 & page 15)
1. a) 1.06   b) 1.17
2. 1   −7   −31
3. a) 14.5 cm   b) 2.65 kg
c) $5\frac{1}{4}$ m or 5.25 m   d) 6.2 litres
4. a) £2.40   b) €10
5. a) 8   b) 62   c) 60
6. $\frac{2}{3} = \frac{20}{30} = \frac{6}{9} = \frac{14}{21} = \frac{30}{45}$

7.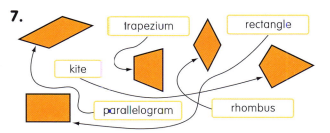

8.

12 hr	24 hr
7:25 am	07:25
7:50 pm	19:50
3:32 pm	15:32
10:39 am	10:39

9. 14,057
10. 4850

Unit 11: Properties of numbers (page 16)
1. a) 136   b) 4314   c) 4124   d) 3509
2. a)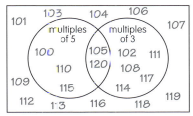

b)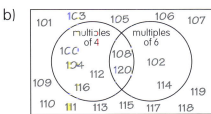

3. 360 can be exactly divided by: 2, 3, 4, 5, 6, 9 and 10

Unit 12: Area and perimeter (page 17)
1. a) 28 cm²   22 cm
b) 54 cm²   30 cm
c) 20 cm²   18 cm
d) 24 cm²   22 cm
e) 18 cm²   22 cm
f) 84 cm²   40 cm
g) 108 cm²   42 cm
h) 72 cm²   34 cm
2. a) perimeter = 24 cm   area = 36 cm²
b) 36 cm   c) 144 cm²

Unit 13: Multiplication (page 18)
1. a) 120   b) 400   c) 180   d) 180
152   456   192   186
e) 420
444

31

2. a) 237   b) 504   c) 380
    d) 376   e) 567

3. a) 34.2 cm^2 b) 23.5 cm^2
    c) 20.4 cm^2 d) 73.6 cm^2

Unit 14: Division (page 19)

1. a) 81 r2   b) 77 r1   c) 47 r1
    d) 87   e) 73 r2   f) 51 r4
    g) 34 r2   h) 132 r1   i) 162 r2

2. a) 116 and 780   b) 780 and 425
    c) 780 and 762   d) 425 and 677
    e) 677 and 762   f) 116, 677 and 425

3. a)   b)

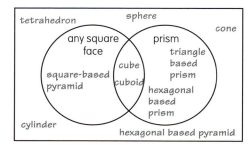

Unit 15: 3D shapes (page 20)

1.

Shape	a)	b)	c)	d)	e)	f)	g)	h)
Prism	✓			✓		✓		✓
Pyramid		✓	✓		✓		✓	

2.

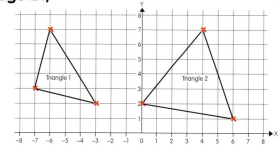

Unit 16: Position and direction (page 21)

1.

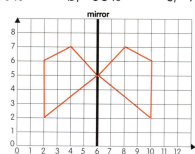

2. a) A → (−2, 8) B → (6, 4)
    b) parallelogram

Unit 17: Decimals (page 22)

1. a) 0.4   b) 0.7   c) 0.125
    d) 0.8   e) 0.625

2. a) $\frac{9}{10}$ b) $\frac{3}{10}$ c) $\frac{17}{20}$ d) $\frac{3}{20}$ e) $\frac{1}{100}$

3. 3.2 → $3\frac{1}{5}$ 2.8 → $2\frac{4}{5}$
    3.5 → $3\frac{1}{2}$ 2.7 → $2\frac{7}{10}$
    3.4 → $3\frac{2}{5}$ 2.75 → $2\frac{3}{4}$

    3.25 → $3\frac{1}{4}$ 2.125 → $2\frac{1}{8}$

Unit 18: Percentages (page 23)

1. a) 70%   b) 75%   c) 80%
    d) 68%   e) 95%   f) 60%
    g) 15%   h) 92%

2. a) 3   b) 1   c) 3
    d) 9   e) 9   f) 1
    g) 3   h) 49

3. a) 1%   b) 80%   c) 80%
    d) 70%   e) 72%   f) 80%

Unit 19: Symmetry (page 24)

1. Check the triangle drawn has these coordinates: (7 , 3) (11 , 1) (10 , 8)

2. Check the first quadrilateral has been plotted correctly.
The reflected quadrilateral coordinates: (5 , 1) (8 , 0) (5 , 3) (2 , 0)

3. The reflected pentagon coordinates: (7 , 0) (4 , 0) (1 , 2) (4, 4) (7 , 4)

Unit 20: Money (page 25)

1. a) £22.99   b) £19.49
    c) £22.79   d) £5.85
    e) £14.79   f) £3.19

2. They need to visit 8 times.

Full-time check-up test (page 26 & page 27)

1. 144 ← 276   216

2. area = 91 cm^2
    perimeter = 40 cm

3. a) 304   b) 43.2

4. a) 72 r4   b) 138 r3

5. a) odd one out = squared based pyramid, the rest are prisms
    b) odd one out = triangle based prism, the rest are pyramids

6. A → (−5, 3)   B → (0, 5)

7. a) 0.6   b) $\frac{1}{4}$
    c) 0.7   d) $\frac{1}{50}$ (or $\frac{2}{100}$)

8. a) 60%   b) 35%   c) 78%

9.

10. £7.27